STUDIES
IN TRANSLATION

by

Valerie Wu

2018

Printed in the United States of America

First Printing, 2018

ISBN 978-0-578-21157-2

Front cover image by Valerie Wu

Wu Publishing
20040 Sea Gull Way
Saratoga, CA 95070

www.valeriewu.org

TABLE OF CONTENTS

PERSONAL ESSAY

CHINATOWNS

Originally constructed in San Jose, California's Heilenville Chinatown in 1888, the Chinese American Museum at the Ng Shing Gung began as a community center, hosting lessons on Chinese calligraphy and literature. Also known as the Temple of the Five Gods, the building served a dual purpose as a hostel for travelers. Many frequented the center; it was a reminder of ethnic unity in the face of racism outside its boundaries. To some, Chinatown was a "safe space," a place where people looked like them and spoke their language. Culture formed connection.

However, by the 1930s, many of Heilenville's original residents passed away. The remaining population was composed of primarily second-generation and third-generation immigrants, who soon left the community in order to seek better career opportunities elsewhere. With the Chinese Exclusion Act preventing new arrivals from China, the Heilenville estate quickly fell to bankruptcy and the surrounding area was razed by the City of San Jose.

In 1949, the Ng Shing Gung was destroyed by the city to clear the area for development. Forty-two years later, the Chinese Historical Cultural Project replicated the original temple, restoring it as a community center. Since then, the temple has housed the Chinese American Historical Museum.

The museum chronicles the saga of Chinese and Chinese Americans living in the Santa Clara Valley.

Exhibitions include the original gilded altar from 1888,
statues of the five Gods, and a film screening of Home
Base: A Chinatown Called Heilenville, about the history
of San Jose's Chinatown and its residents. Through
providing exposure to the area's ethnic heritage, this
remnant of historical Chinatown's vibrant community
strives to preserve cultural legacies. Although based in
San Jose, the museum tells a collective narrative of
resistance, resilience, and recovery for the Chinese
community in the United States today.

————

The first time I came to New York's Chinatown was
because I had seen a cheap, authentic dumpling place
via Yelp. My family and I had been in New York for a
week, and meals had consisted of burgers and
gourmet cuisine and afternoon tea at the Plaza--
American things, but not Chinese things. We were
desperate for Asian food. We wanted yellow people
and yellow restaurants and *mai yi song yi* and people
who looked like us, talked like us. We bought thirty-
six of those dumplings to-go, wrapped them in a
plastic bag with a yellow smiley-face that said thank
you, and took the subway back to our hotel.

The dumplings were good, but what I couldn't help
thinking about was the people who made them. From
the beginning, Chinatowns have always existed as a
form of unity for yellow people. Back in San
Francisco, the street's looming gates signified much
more than just a place, but a community. It was funny
when you thought about it, because people always
thought of Chinese food as kung pao chicken and

Chinese girls as china dolls, the kinds you'd see in dollar shops down the alley--innocent and voiceless-- an ethnic theme park.

What I didn't fully understand then was that these communities don't exist for the purpose of another individual's learning experience. They--we--exist because of our own selves, because we embrace and understand our culture--all the social practices and customs that come with it. Because we have roots back home and we'll always be tied to them, in some shape or form. Because we remember where we came from, and we'll never forget it.

The Chinatown I went to in New York was just like the ones you'd see anywhere else, except behind the signs with Chinese characters and the five-dollar qipao, there were New York buildings, the kind you see on phone screens and wallpapers. The American Dream loomed over the city, big and bright. There was Golden Wok take-out, an acupuncture clinic down the street, an Asian woman talking to her son on the phone—*no, go do your Physics homework. AP exam coming up, you want to get a five or not?*

This was our own little home, underneath the Manhattan skyline. Here, there was a yellow rhythm. We knew that beat, were uniquely familiar with it. It was my first time in New York's Chinatown, but it wasn't the first time I understood what a place meant to the people who lived there. One of my mother's friends from Silicon Valley moved to Long Island last year, near Queens. She'd gone to Stanford too, just like everyone else in the neighborhood. I'd never really known her daughter that well, but we'd both liked milk tea. (While she liked the kind with grass jelly and more sugar, I preferred the ones with salted cheese.) We had debates about the kinds of drinks we liked in both Taiwan and America, the way each was made differently when it came from a different place. We thought about drinks the way we did about people, hyphenated. When the family left, I didn't really feel anything. If I did, I didn't know what word to use at the time. But sometimes I'd pass by their house and would feel something eating at me inside, leaving a hole no amount of sugar could ever fill.

A white couple moved into their house the following week. I watched them as the moving van arrived and observed what they brought in: patterned placemats and marble tables and televisions--American things-- but no rice cooker, Chinese things.

We visited my mother's friend in Queens a while ago over noodles and milk tea, in a little Chinese plaza in Flushing. She told us that everything was different on the East Coast, and not just the weather. It was the people and the place, she said. Because sure, Asians were aggressive in Silicon Valley, but back there everyone knew each other and who came from where—*oh, I'm from Miaoli, so that's close*—and in New York, people were cold, distant. It was difficult for people from different boroughs to understand one another. Everyone was always following up on the American Dream, the promises of purple mountains majesty and Ivy League schools.

We asked her if she would ever want to go back. She said no, not really. Maybe it was time to move on. But she'd still go to Asian supermarkets and get take-out noodles, the authentic kind, and make dumplings out of meat and dough from the grocery store. It was her way of reassuring herself that she was still being understood.

Sometimes I wonder about what the Chinatowns mean to all us who migrate, who move from place to place and never really know where we belong. I'm wondering if someone will ever take the time to walk into Chinatown and think about what it means to those who crave Asian food, who scroll through Yelp to find real, authentic places to eat at. I'm wondering if someone will ever try to understand the four tones—the rising and the falling, the flat and the one that I still can't get into words—the comma, the sound of something still unfinished.

The first thing my mother did after coming to Stanford was join the Taiwanese Students Association, just because she knew that there would be people who knew what she was talking about when she said *mifen* (rice noodles) and the distance from *Ximen* to *Danshui*. This is just one of the many stories of resistance in America: the way ethnic communities preserve and uphold one another, the way we resemble those yellow plastic smiles when we find someone who looks like us and talks like us. I see you, our smiles say, I see you.

The Chinatown in New York looks just like the ones anywhere else. The streets may be different, but the concept is the same. I don't know if it's possible to visualize race in America in another way than the communities that shape it. Maybe Chinatowns are diluted in some way, lost in their traditions. But they'll never be ghosts. They'll always exist for those who need them.

Before we left Flushing, my mother told her friend that if she ever needed anything, she was always free to come back. The places would still be the same. Silicon Valley would still be Silicon Valley; San Jose would still be San Jose. The same Chinese, Japanese, and Korean restaurants would still be there. It'd be authentic just as long as there were people around to keep it that way, to preserve the narrative. I wasn't sure if the words meant something to her.

When she smiled, though, it was big and bright, yellow. Thank you, she seemed to say, thank you.

WORKS CITED

Bryant, Dale. "The Chinese American Museum at History Park San Jose Celebrates 20 Years." The Mercury News. October 06, 2011. Accessed September 18, 2018.
https://www.mercurynews.com/2011/10/06/the-chinese-american-museum-at-history-park-san-jose-celebrates-20-years/.

"CAHMuseum." Chinese Historical and Cultural Project Website. July 14, 2018. Accessed September 18, 2018. http://chcp.org/cah-museum/.

"Chinese American Historical Museum at the Ng Shing Gung." Chinese Historical and Cultural Project Website. July 14, 2018. Accessed September 18, 2018. http://chcp.org/cah-museum/.

Liberation Space: Race and Memory in a Nation Divided

One perceives memory in many different ways.

War memory is one type of memory, the politics of it. It is created in the communities of color that are uniquely victim to wars of nationalism. In the wake of events such as Japanese American internment in World War II and the First Indochina War between France, the colonizer, and Vietnam, the colonized, war memory is perpetuated in the stories we tell: the narrative experiences of those who were persecuted because of the color of their skin or the name they were given by their parents, and those who bear witness to the legacies of ethnic prejudice.

The experience of each nation shapes its politics of memory. In America, history calls it the Vietnam War. In Vietnam, history calls it the American War. In America, history calls it the Korean War. In Korea, history calls it the Fatherland Liberation War. History gives our memories their names before we can claim them ourselves. This selective perception of events is influenced by the divisions between what we see and what we want to see.

Yet there are other sides to memory as well--the memories we tell ourselves, and the memories we teach our children.

When I first took AP United States History, I became distinctly aware of the deliberate exclusion of Asian American memories from a Western lens. In our discussions of Japanese American internment, America's concentration camps were perceived as simply Korematsu v. United States (1944), with an emphasis on the United States. We failed to evaluate the social implications behind the incarceration of Japanese Americans. Internees were numbers. Statistics were our primary sources. These differences in perceptions affect how we view ethnic minority groups as a whole.

This seemingly deliberate "gap of consciousness" reflected my understanding of race in America. In a nation where I could not even communicate with those who looked like me in my textbook, I did not understand why I was still being told "go back to your country." When United States History told me that internment was constitutional with Executive Order 9066, but failed to explain its legacies, I did not--could not--understand why racism still existed, or why one side was still viewed as "alien" and the other was not.

Today, when we look at ethnic communities, we find that differences in perception color the conceptions of race in America. The perspective that Japanese Americans are a threat to the security of America has prevented the United States from achieving full equality. In a nation where Asian Americans are still hitting the glass ceiling because of the name on their resumes and facing discrimination--physically and verbally--because of the color of their skin, the deliberate exclusion and erasure of Asian Americans in our history textbooks has had an undeniable effect in that process.

As the second-generation daughter of immigrants, this invisibility is a reality for me. My goal is to combat this through the stories we tell, and in effect, shift our perspectives on the politics of memory, starting with our history textbooks.

During the summer before junior year, I began working with POC (People of Color) Online Classroom to curate a collection of education resources on Asian American identity and social history. The organization, first founded in November 2016, was created to assist both people of color and allies in learning about the multiracial communities that exist today. Titled "Model Minority Mutiny," the syllabus is a compilation of Asian American voices in historical and global context. The project is based off the idea that only by rewriting--our "rerighting"--our history can we become more informed on what we can do to alleviate race relations in our role as citizens of America.

"Model Minority Mutiny" is a journey into the very annals of Asian American history. From the construction of San Francisco's first "Oriental School" in 1885 to the 1966 New York Times article that labeled Japanese Americans as the "model minority," the history presented throughout is aimed at an Asian American audience. As human rights activist Yuri Kochiyama said, "Unless we know ourselves and our history, and other people and their history, there is really no way we can really have positive kind of interaction where there is mutual understanding."

This incorporation of Asian American voices is designed to spark conversations about the way we see Asian Americans today--not just as numbers and statistics, but individuals with voices that are just as valuable as the voices of any other ethnic group in America.

Since the publication of "Model Minority Mutiny," the curriculum has reached an international audience. Its resources will be used in the exhibit In(di)visible at the Station Museum in Houston, a curation of the (East/Southeast) Asian American experience across history. We've received feedback from students who are planning to petition their schools' history departments for its inclusion in their curriculums. Through conversations with those I've worked with to implement the voices of the revolt in my community, I've learned that race is both a way of reiterating our humanity as much as it is seeing it for ourselves.

The memories ethnic minorities retain of their own authentic experiences are a liberation space. Memories will always be political. The existence of Asian Americans in the America of today will always be political. Here, the boundaries between countries blur. Race is not a singular narrative, but a collective one.

As a minority, I have seen racism. I have seen teachers who have said that my words aren't my own because my parents are immigrants. I have seen the microaggressions of the contemporary classroom-- being called the same name as another Asian, being told that I "look like the enemy" while learning about communism in China, being categorized according to the profile of an Asian American: good at math, voiceless, without dreams of my own. These are differences in perception that ultimately affect not only minorities, but contribute to ignorance in America.

How we perceive history is affected by how we write it. Just like the experiences of each nation shapes the politics of memory, the experiences of each individual does as well.

When we give the platform of American history to those who have been mistreated by it, we give ourselves the social and political freedom to tell our own stories. We become our own heroes. We revolutionize our own conversations. We create our own spaces for liberation. We reclaim our own narratives, one story at a time.

Mitosis

[PROPHASE]

The pre-med girls walked down the street every morning.

But they weren't pre-med, at least not yet. They liked thinking that they were, though; they liked talking about saving lives--it totally wasn't about the success or anything like that--they liked it when their parents introduced them to other Asian parents with: "Oh, this is my daughter. She's pre-med." And then the other parents would smile, grin, say, "Oh, your daughter is so accomplished. She's going to do great things."

Because pre-med was a great term, a brilliant term that all the Asians in town wore like a Science Olympiad gold medal. Asian girls liked talking about the kinds of stories you'd read about in novels: late-night football games, high school proms, Mean Girls. But they'd never been to football games. Their high school proms were sitting on benches and finishing up Calculus homework. The only mean girls were the ones who glared at you after the bell rang and you'd finished your test and they hadn't. These were the little details, the little things that pre-med girls admired--even fawned over--but didn't fully understand.

When I was younger, my grandfather ran a skin care clinic in Taiwan. We lived upstairs from the clinic each summer. In the mornings we'd come down, watch as my grandfather looked at one person's foot, the back of a neck, a hand: intimate parts, fleshed-out parts. I'd watch from the worn-out leather stool in the corner. The little plastic fan attached to the sink never worked, and my shorts were always sticking to my thighs.

There was a man--a regular customer--who came to the clinic every week. He had some sort of fungus on his foot, and he'd always stick his foot up on my grandfather's table. "See," he'd say in sputtering Mandarin, "Still there!" His sandal would slip off sometimes, and I'd sometimes get a glimpse of what lay beneath before it was covered up by my grandfather's hand. Let me help you, my grandfather would say. His eyes would shine, and in that instant there would be a visible sigh of the man's shoulders, as if he'd just realized that this man--this doctor who knew medicine, the art of healing--could save his life.

Every Christmas, we'd have boxes shipped to our home from Taiwan, the bold Mandarin stickers taped to the front: fragile, handle with care. There were tiny ziploc bags of pretty pills and tablets, tubes of cream. I'd always wondered what it meant to have a grandfather who packed pills in bags and wrapped medicinal powders in tissue paper. Each one had its own unique name--the Chinese characters stuck to the bottles. And sometimes they were named just like American names: amphetamine, methylphenidate, vivalin. Other times they were labeled after the purposes they served. *Zhang gao* meant to grow

17

taller. *Tou tung* was migraine. *Wen zi* yao was bug bites. There was something inexplicably beautiful about the names, the way words formulated prescriptions and prescriptions translated to reshaping, reforming.

"Why do you do this?" I'd asked my grandfather once. He'd grown up in the basement of a fabric shop, where rats were always found dead under the piano and poverty was a given. It wasn't until he decided to open his own medicine clinic that the fabric shop became an apartment. The apartment became a four-story building. I'd always assumed that the reason he chose to go into medicine was for the success.

My grandfather had looked at me as if he couldn't believe that was even a question. "To save lives," he'd replied.

In that instant I was reminded of the countless other pre-med girls who had said these exact same words, that I want to save lives, as if those words meant something.

What hurt was that I could have been one of those pre-med girls. I wasn't really good at math, but I'd done science fair. I hadn't won anything, but that was okay. What mattered was doing it and talking to those around me: girls who had been doing science for as long as they could remember, girls who designed apps that solved third-world problems, girls who purified water with the formulas inside their heads, girls whose inventions were so, so much realer than themselves.

[METAPHASE]

The first time I ever participated in science fair, I began to split apart.

I'd dressed up specifically for the occasion. As I walked to the convention center, I hitched my board to my waist, feeling professional and powerful. It was a glorious feeling, being pre-med. Maybe this was what the pre-med girls felt like every day. Now I was one of them.

We had all received badges when we entered the auditorium for the science fair; each one listed how many years we'd been participating. I only had one blue dot, but there was an Indian girl next to me who had nine. Her board looked professional, like she had spent hundreds of dollars designing it. She'd connected all these wires to it. The front of the board said her name, big and bold and blue. Her pantsuit made her look like she was running for office, rather than attending a science fair. She wore all the medals she'd received from previous years around her neck, as if to say: I'm experienced. I know how to win. I'm pre-med.

I would have loved to be her at that moment: poised, calm, confident. But then I saw how unhappy she looked. Her project was on trying to find a cure for the developmental stages of cancer, a continuation. She'd done research all for the past few years just to find the cure for cancer. Her dad had come with her, carrying a piece of equipment. He was beaming like she'd just gotten into Harvard. (She probably would.) They came to the table across from my measly-looking board on learning languages, and set everything down with such an alarming speed that it was clear this was just another day to them.

For the remainder of the fair, I watched as the girl spoke to wide-eyed competitors, people who had come with goggles and electrical equipment and things that screamed power, success, and changing the world, one invention at a time. "Yeah, curing cancer," she'd say, "I'm coming really close to it. Should be a few more months."

I stood by my project, feeling awkward and ordinary, but most of all not pre-med. Because I'd probably never be pre-med. I'd probably never find the cure for cancer. I'd never be someone who invented things that were realer than myself.

An old white lady passed by--a judge, presumably. The girl stood up, straightened her suit, prepared for a discussion. The lady looked at her and frowned. I watched as she grilled the girl on her project, asked if she really thought she was going to cure cancer, asked why she felt like it was her place to conduct such an experiment.

And the girl just kept on stating the same fact, the same I want to save lives. I just want to save lives. She said it so methodically that I began wondering if she really wanted to save lives at all, or if it was more of the feeling of being pre-med, the feeling of power, of success--feeling like you were someone to be proud of. Not just a collection of cells, but a complete, full, whole human being: someone who could save the world, but not someone who was real.

I checked the winners list a few weeks later. She had gotten first place.

[ANAPHASE]

Top student Laura Zhang committed suicide on a Wednesday in December.

That was the headline: top student before her name, as if it was expected that academic excellence would always take precedent over just another Asian, just another one of those pre-med girls, accomplished daughters, people who were going to do great things.

They say she lay there on the railroad until the train came. That she didn't open her eyes, not once. That her biology textbook stayed right next to her until the end, flipped to a page on mitosis because she had a test on cell division the next day. She'd always been fascinated by splitting apart that it wasn't so surprising she decided to do it herself.

I'd never really known Laura Zhang, except that she and the pre-med girls were always walking down the street across school. They were good with the whitening cream. They ordered boba at the milk tea shop downtown. It was always the same, perfect ratio: regular size, seventy-five percent ice and twenty-five percent sugar. One of the pre-med girls would chew one-sided while talking about plasma membranes and looking through an electron transmission microscope. The other would be reading a chapter on cellular respiration. Laura, though, stood out. She was the one who was always talking about saving lives, just saving lives and helping people, the kind of medicine that mattered. Her eyes would shine.

About a week after her death, we learned Laura Zhang had been taking Adderall. They'd found the pills in the front pocket of her backpack; she'd overdosed on the night of her death. *Probably because of the AP Biology final tomorrow*, we said. *It was just the stress*, we said. *Familial pressure*, we said. We joked. *Pre-med gone wrong*, we said. What we really wanted to know was why. Was there something else going on we didn't know about?

Truth was, I don't think we ever really understood why Laura died the way she did. We always thought about her like chemotherapy--a source of healing. She was the pre-med girl who every mother wanted her daughter to be like, the perfect one. Back then, we never realized that she was the cancerous cell in all of us: the internalized self-hatred, the anxiety of trying to follow a path we'd never fully understand, the bitterness of a pill past its expiration date.

Laura Zhang always talked about saving lives. But in the days and weeks after her death, I began to think that maybe she was so focused on saving other people's lives that she forgot about her own.

[TELOPHASE]

My mother drove me past my old college prep center in December, a year since Laura Zhang's death and an hour after my last final exam of the semester. The window was rolled down and in that brief second, I could hear murmurs of conversation: *I have a violin competition this week* and *I don't think this SAT score is good enough for the Ivies* and *I'm already taking three sciences, but another one wouldn't hurt.*

There used to be flyers that would hang on the windows listing the center's alumnae and their college majors. Three-quarters of the sheets said Biology. I remembered how Asian parents would cling to those sheets as if they were lifelines. When the center faded from view, I couldn't help thinking about how we'd all been clinging to those dreams like lifelines.

In the small, Asian American community I'd grown up in, you either knew what you were going to be or you didn't. Whenever someone asked you how you were doing, you'd reply with I'm doing fine, how about you? You knew who you were. There was no undecided. Pre-med was brilliant, a glorious thing you'd wear around your neck like a Science Olympiad gold medal.

The thing was, I would never be one of those pre-med girls. I liked my milk tea regular size, but with seventy-five percent sugar and twenty-five percent ice. I'd never won science fair. I'd probably never be someone who invented things that were realer than myself.

My mother turned to face me in her seat, as if the college prep center had reminded her that I was a student too. "How did your exam go?" she asked.

Briefly I thought back to how it had went: monomers, polymers, things that would string together to form bigger things. Proteins were made up of amino acids. There were hydrogen bonds, peptide bonds, and covalent and ionic bonds. Mitosis was the repeated division of the cell. And I knew that what my mother wanted to hear wasn't about biology and the processes that formed them, but whether or not I'd make her proud, give her something to tell the other parents--something that they'd smile at, say: "Oh, your daughter is so accomplished. She's going to do great things."

Across the street, the pre-med girls were entering the boba shop, biology textbooks in arm. I watched as two of them went inside, perfect genomic replicas of one another. The third one stood outside for a while, staring through the window. She opened her backpack and slipped the textbook in. And then she walked the other way, and I wasn't sure how to react, except that this--this was real, and this was mitosis in action, cells splitting apart and reforming again.

24

"I don't know," I admitted. "I really don't know."

[CYTOKINESIS]

In biology, mitosis is defined as the type of cell
division that results in two identical daughter cells.
These cells have the same number of chromosomes.
They contain the same genes and the same
replications of those genes. They are identical copies
of one another.

What many of us didn't understand was that saving
lives in concept is much different from saving lives in
practice. Because saving lives wasn't just pills and
powders; it wasn't just talking about it. It was
knowing that this was your purpose. It was knowing
that throughout all the phases of your life, this was
what you wanted to do. It was knowing that the cycle
would start again, and this time you'd be an intrinsic
part of it.

There are two different types of mitosis: closed and
open. In a "closed mitosis"--the kind that fungi
undergo--chromosomes are only dividing within a
nucleus. It's limited. In an "open mitosis"--the kind
animal cells undergo--the nuclear envelope has
already broken down before the chromosomes
separate. There are no more restrictions.

The last stage, cytokinesis, overlaps with the final stages. That's when the daughter cells split apart, reform again. No matter the mitosis, though, the cells are the same: always dividing and developing, regenerating and replacing. There will always be parents who introduce their daughters to others, saying: "Oh, this is my daughter." And there will always be unspoken questions. *Why do you do what you do? Why is it your place to conduct such an experiment? Is there something else going on that we don't know about? What's your major?*

What will you be?

TIGER, DREAMING

Tigers are part of the kingdom *Animalia*, phylum *Chordata*, class *Carnivora*. They belong to the family of Felidae; they are part of the genus Panthera. A tiger's ancestry can be traced using genetic analysis and tracing the phylogenetic relationships between its evolutionary relatives. Once, I dreamed of a tiger and ran my hand through its fur, felt potential thrumming within its veins, felt the inherent wildness deep within its heart.

My mother often spoke to me of hidden potential, the kind that lies deep within you. It's the palpable kind of potential that thrives in the territory it's claimed. I was good at piano within a range of notes, but I had the potential to become better outside of that range. Taiwan had opportunities, but there were more opportunities in America. Opportunity and potential are distinctly related; they can be traced exponentially. Substantiation and self-worth are transparent, an invisible line. Draw a punnett square, you'll find that there's no escaping the need to pursue self-actualization in each generation. The X will always have an exponent attached.

In Silicon Valley, the kids are made of matter, the kind of matter that exists only in liquid form. They conform to fit their environment. You can try diluting their yellowness, but they'll keep reacting, keep combusting, keep making products. Sometimes, there's so much orange that one often forgets that there are stripes at all. All of us bleed red, the red of opportunity, the red of the American Dream, the red of orange on our skin, tanned from the California sun. Once, I played the piano for an hour each night, wanting to achieve something, something more than letters on a sheet of paper--because I believed in potential, and I believed in achieving a territory of self-worth. We laughed at our tiger mothers, mothers who made us do at least twenty math problems a day and play the piano for three hours each night, but truth was, we believed in our potential just as much as they did. Regarding her book Battle Hymn of the Tiger Mother, Amy Chua describes her parenting style as a firm belief in the power of pushing her children to their fullest potential; it was the principle we were all founded on.

I was never a particularly bright student--I wasn't smart in the way others were, I didn't ever truly get things the way others understood them. Most of the time, I just couldn't remember facts, and grammar rules, and didn't look at teachers with a spark of intelligence. I was just there, a presence that no one really knew what to make of. So I pushed myself to become better, because I knew that that was what my mother wanted me to be: the most exceptional version of myself I could be. While others spent one hour studying for the upcoming math test, I spent three. There were ratios in my ability to perform and my ability to work hard enough to perform better. And I knew that it was this orange that characterized me, but for me it was more than that. It was the willingness and capacity to grow. It was American progress, the Manifest Destiny of there always being room for expansion, room to move until one could settle in the right spot.

The "model minority" doesn't exist, but the work ethic does. Many have misunderstood the drive, the motivation, that immigrants have in a country not their own. Because yes, it was about getting good grades, and knowing how to do math problems, and playing an instrument, but it was also the concept of opportunity, the desire for meaning. Talking about tiger moms may seem like a joke, but I've come to understand it as the belief in potential. We've come to associate discipline with oppression; that's not the case. The kids in Silicon Valley just want to matter. They dream of mattering in the scope of the world, and I think people have often misconstrued that to the point where it's become ambiguous.

I live in Silicon Valley, a community of immigrants. Our mothers pushed us as far as we could go, and even then, farther. I remember my days as a child, wondering why the things I accomplished--the tests I'd scored well on--were never enough. But I realize now that we, the second-generation, are the products of dreams. We'll always keep reacting, keep combusting, keep making products, because it's why our parents came here--so we would have the opportunity to. Inherent wildness lies within us; when someone breaks us apart into our simple compounds, the essence of our multiple components, they'll see our stripes and know what it means--that we're tigers, dreaming. Because being orange isn't just a state of being; it's a kingdom, a phylum, a family. It's an individual, it's a people, it's a nation.

RESEARCH PAPER

THE RACIAL IMAGINARY IN A-BOMB LITERATURE: CONSIDERING THE ROLE OF VICTIM CONSCIOUSNESS IN WAR MEMORY

REISCHAUER SCHOLARS PROGRAM 2018, STANFORD UNIVERSITY

The atomic bombings of Hiroshima and Nagasaki on August 6 and 9, 1945, respectively, are commonly regarded as the prime example of nuclear atrocities committed by one country for the deliberate purpose of harming another. In the comprehensive history of nuclear warfare, Japan is the only country to have ever experienced the atomic bomb. The strong attitudes of the Japanese toward denuclearization in the Asia-Pacific region continue today because of this, as well as a desire to promote peace and conflict resolution, as shown by former U.S. president Barack Obama's visits to the Hiroshima Peace Memorial.

Yet remnants of differing war memories concerning the Pacific War exist in the aesthetic and social postwar narratives of race, most explicitly in the preservation of the theory of "Asian suffering," or Japan's vulnerability to American socio-political interests (Glosserman). Using literature of the time period, it is critical to understand their effects on Japanese national identity as indicative of the need for denuclearization efforts, but also their role in Japan's evasion of responsibility for wartime actions and the importance of countering Japan's dominant narrative of victim consciousness.

Victim consciousness is commonly defined as the inability to take responsibility for one's actions during wartime and instead focus on the immoral repercussions of war. Evidence of victim consciousness persists in the legacies of the atomic bombings, as represented in literature produced by Japanese authors during and after the time period. Called *genbaku bungaku*, or "atomic bomb literature" in English, these narratives on the Pacific War integrate cross-cultural conceptions of race relations in order to provide a voice for *hibakusha*, the survivors of the atomic bombings. As constructed in the racial imaginary defined in transnational narratives of the Pacific War, Japanese literary responses to the United States' bombings of Hiroshima and Nagasaki illuminate the rise of generational trauma through war memory in order to reinforce the dehumanization of the Japanese people and perpetuate victim consciousness as a fundamental part of Japanese identity.

Historical Context of the Atomic Bombs

Firstly, background of the atomic bombings is needed in order to fully comprehend how it impacted the chronicling of the incidents in historical memory. Original development and deployment of the atomic bombings were rationalized through an American lens of racial superiority, which contributed to the cultural conflict that featured most prominently in the Japanese narratives that followed. Dehumanization of the Japanese in the United States began with anti-immigration/racist sentiment, particularly demonstrated in the "Yellow Peril" movement characterizing those of Asian ethnicities as animalistic and socially inferior (Yang). This anti-Japanese rhetoric was only sustained by the "Remember Pearl Harbor" slogan after Japan's attacks on Pearl Harbor; because memories of Japanese atrocities influenced American perceptions of Japan, the United States wanted to demonstrate nuclear power over the country—a type of biological and psychological warfare against a race deemed to be subordinate.

Later, Japan's writers of the atomic bomb would capitalize on this element of dehumanization and use it to further their narratives of Japan's victimization in the Asia-Pacific War. Thus, reasons behind the decisions to drop the atomic bombs were affected by the aesthetics of race ideologies and enabled the United States to ethicize what would otherwise be unethical acts. American narratives pursued a false reality in their justification of the atomic bombings as a "necessary evil," which Japanese literature of the atomic bombs later recapitulated and deconstructed as a way of reinforcing victim consciousness.

Yet racialization of American atrocities was in the choice of where to deploy the bombs as well (Halstead). When American military executives first considered the target of the atomic bombings, the city of Kyoto was an initial focus, as it was considered an "intellectual and cultural" hub of the country (Ham). Reasoning behind the deliberate targeting of a Japanese cultural hub was directly correlated to the racial hierarchy within America. Because the citizens of Japan were perceived as biologically "lesser" during nuclear warfare, the United States' intent was to cause destructive effects on national identity. The idea of Kyoto was later disregarded, as Hiroshima--a city that was both militarily and structurally compact--was chosen as the primary recipient in order to establish American military strength over the citizens of Japan.

This political and racial dominance was at both subconscious and conscious levels; Japanese considerations of American atrocities were subsequently discerned in the fragmentation of Japanese identity in the national psyche. Japanese memories of the atomic bombings assigned responsibility to the United States and failed to recognize the Japanese atrocities that had been committed during wartime (e.g. "comfort women," colonial violence, the Nanjing Massacre). Japan, gripped by the pacifist sentiments of "ban the bomb" fever, focused on political campaigns involving the landlords/individuals whose livelihoods were destroyed by the atomic bombings, but most specifically the hibakusha, who were believed to have the most relevant narratives to portraying Japan as the victim (Orr 17). Later, their narratives were inscribed into the canon of historical literature surrounding U.S.-Japan relations, further perpetuating Japan's victim consciousness.

Atomic Bomb Literature and Memories

Depictions of generational trauma by hibakusha during the period after the atomic bombings argued primarily that nuclear warfare was a means of dehumanization and justified Japan's victimhood. As historian John Dower writes, "Hiroshima and Nagasaki became icons of Japanese suffering— perverse national treasures, of a sort, capable of fixating Japanese memory of the war on what had happened to Japan and simultaneously blotting out the recollection of the Japanese victimization of others" (144). Nowhere was this represented more than in genbaku bungaku, which conveyed a spectrum of experiences of both survivors and those who were indirectly impacted by the atomic bombs.

The genre of A-bomb literature can be separated into three classes representative of the phases after the atomic bombings: 1) personal accounts of the effects of the atomic bombings (social), 2) third-person narratives of victim consciousness (psychological), and 3) journalistic analyses drawing on various sources to provide a reference point for the future of denuclearization (political). Each narrative segment of history serves to illustrate the intersection of ethnicity and humanity, and together, provides a cohesive argument as to how the Japanese were the victims of nuclear warfare. Literary fragmentation seen in these works translated to the "fragmentation" of ethnic/cultural collectivist identity in the period afterwards (Tan).

Personal Accounts: Social Narratives

One poem that exemplifies this phenomenon in the first class of genbaku bungaku is "This is a human being?" (1950) by well-known Japanese author Tamiki Hara, whose writing chronicles the immediate effects of the atomic bombings. Much of his poetry characterizes the atomic bombings as causing both physical and mental damage. The atomic bomb is portrayed as an inhumane device representative of American racial attitudes towards the Japanese, and a calculated attack on Japanese national identity.

In the poem, Hara states: "This is a human being? Look how the atom bomb changed it. / Flesh swells fearfully. / All men and women take one shape. / The voice that trickles from swollen lips...this is the face of a human being" (Hara). His literary focus here is the atomic bomb's damage on Japanese citizens. When he states that men and women take "one shape," he is referring to the Japanese becoming "faceless" as a result of the inhumanity of nuclear warfare, a direct conduit to the dehumanization of a people. Commencing with an emphasis on the biological effects of the atomic bombings, Hara then transitions to a discussion of physical and spiritual associations. The metaphysical nature of hibakusha becomes a platform for reiterating the humanity of Japanese victims, a memory of war that ultimately surfaced in Japanese perceptions of American reasoning behind the atrocities.

Third-Person Accounts: Psychological

Following the literature written by hibakusha, the generational divide between those who survived the atomic bombings and those whose lives were affected was displayed in the second genre of genbaku bungaku. Focusing on autobiographical narratives, works like Urashimaso by Minako Oba served to underscore past narrative experiences of the atomic bombings. For instance, Urashimaso (1977) has often been described as a "counter-memory, a subjective and individualized recollection of the war" (Tachibana 197). Oba was inspired to write the novel after her experiences with hibakusha, but wanted to reshape the perspectives involved in the war and fictionalize the narrative in order to demystify certain ambiguities of the atomic bombings.

Urashimaso is a blend of reality and fantasy. Using images from popular Japanese folktales and culture, the novel centers on a non-hibakusha protagonist who travels home to Japan after an extended time away, only to find that the city of Hiroshima has been destroyed by an atomic bomb. This fictionalization of fact is seen in the book's autobiographical elements. Although Oba was at a safe distance from the city when the atomic bombings happened, she later provided care for them as part of a school program. During this time, she stated that she was horrified at the intentional use of the atomic bombs and the subsequent damage that occurred.

In the context of the novel's relationships, the Americans are portrayed as the oppressor and aggressor, while the Japanese are the oppressed victims. In accordance with trauma theory (the idea that an external threat surpasses internal and external resources), the motivation of race was present. In the midst of conflict with the setting, the protagonist is also at conflict with herself as she struggles to explore her own identity in juxtaposition with the identities of others and how they communicate. Such literature was reflective of Japanese cultural conflict and ease in attributing the loss of nationalism to the atomic bombings. In Japanese society, the damage caused by the atomic bombs resulted in teachers refusing to show the Japanese national flag or play the national anthem at school assemblies (Naito). Additionally, the categorical nature of the novel's structure in textually defining the role of the "predator" and the "victim" perpetuated an idea of victim consciousness for the Japanese. Conflicting roles in society are emphasized.

Oba's inclusion of characters with dual identities—i.e., Japanese-Americans—becomes more significant when taken into account as a part of war memory. Because this generation of individuals impacted by the atomic bomb is conflicted as to whether to choose the "American" or "Japanese" side, this representation accentuates the idea that America isolated Japanese identity, separating memories between cultures. In this sense, Oba's character is a plot device that represents the evolution of war memory; the legacies of the atomic bombings translate to a bildungsroman that in essence becomes a distinct exploration of cultural, linguistic, and narrative displacements. What this implies is an insecurity of nationality, as Oba's protagonist never fully realizes the true extent to which she is a victim of American racial preeminence. In the novel, the protagonist is unable to identify with either culture in her perception of the bomb's impact.

Journalistic Accounts: Political

Of the third category are more journalistic analyses of the atomic bombings, in which Masuji Ibuse's Black Rain features most prominently. While the story is in itself a novel, it was based off interviews with hibakusha and the devastation caused by nuclear warfare. The central objective is to convey the depth and magnitude of the atomic bombings, with firsthand witnesses as the primary sources. Following the story of a fictional figure named Shigematsu Shizuma, the novel chronicles the everyday lives of the hibakusha and the physical and spiritual uncertainties that existed afterwards. While the events are drawn from statistics and facts about radiation sickness, the effects of the sickness are illustrated through the social exclusion that Shigematsu's niece Yasuko faces as a result of the atomic bombs.

Ibuse maintains distance from the narrative as only the writer, but simultaneously provides a degree of cultural relativity; again, this underscores the humanity of those who were affected by the bombs. In essence, Black Rain is a meditation on the "universal" experience of tragedy. By repealing earlier conceptions of Japanese aggression and focusing instead on Japan's pacifist sentiments, the Japanese people are regarded solely as the victims of an American atrocity. As historian Philip Seaton writes, "Black Rain allowed Hiroshima to stop being solely the iconography of left-wing pacifism and become a national symbol of victimhood" (Seaton 41). When Yasuko is shunned because of her proximity to the "black rain," she becomes an emblem of the consequences of nuclear warfare. Politically, this type of depiction influenced the growth of Japanese pacifism.

As demonstrated by many of the works produced during the time period, A-Bomb literature often focused on describing the political, historical, and psychological impacts of the atomic bombs. Existentialism was stressed as a means of collectivizing both national identity and distinguishing the individual narratives of those who were victims (Treat 46). However, a shared unity in victim consciousness was transferred to the narratives of history textbooks as well.

Textbook Narratives

Whereas United States history textbooks focused primarily on justifying the military necessity of Hiroshima and Nagasaki and the magnitude of American nuclear power, Japanese textbooks took a different stance on the deployment of the bombs. This political and implicitly racial discourse can reveal how each country interprets the events in collective war memory.

History is based on the nature of words used; it is said that in Japanese textbooks, descriptions are commonly "noun-heavy" and "objective." On the other hand, American history textbooks use "colorful, descriptive, and generally verbose" language. Only American narratives contained content on the reasoning and justification behind the bombs. Comparatively, Japanese narratives concentrated on the role of Japan as the victim/hero, most specifically in its inclusion of the stories of hibakusha, as well as those who were affected by the firebombing of other Japanese cities (Braun).

Based on an examination of the context depicted in these textbooks, Japanese textbooks are more likely to lay out the medical and technological implications of the atomic bombs, rather than the military impact. The deliberate inclusion and exclusion of certain events in turn shape the way each nation reacts to the event. From American textbooks, the atomic bombings are still viewed as a demonstration of the United States' military strength against Japan, the inhumane enemy of the time. From the Japanese perspective, the atomic bombings were atrocities committed against human rights. Instead of warranting the bomb as the majority of American narratives did, Japanese narratives chose to show that the atomic bombings had brutal effects by eliciting sympathy from witnesses to the experiences of the hibakusha.

Oral Traditions

More of the Japanese conception of victimhood can be detected in the textual and spatial analyses of the hibakusha's oral traditions. Through interviews with the hibakusha, researchers found that many of them tended to reflect on the physical toll of nuclear warfare, with an emphasis on the fragility of the human condition. Language referred to the "disintegration of the self," as many body parts—the eyes, nose, hands, mouth—were mentioned as physical remnants of the bombs' destructive effects ("Hiroshima Archives"). The magnitude of the bombs were mentioned not as a way of reinforcing military strength as American narratives did, but rather to stress how the bomb decimated a city's population because of its inhumane nature. Japanese narratives in literature and media isolated these experiences in the context of the atomic bombings and used them to evoke a sense of humanity and empathy for those who suffered.

Ultimately, these narratives served to paint Japan as a "war hero" in their consideration of individual fragmentation. The Japanese adopted a sense of postwar victimhood because of the prominence of A-Bomb literature in war memory. Narratives centered around American attacks and the omission of Japanese acts of aggression provoked contemplative responses on Japan's pacifism and the role of rehabilitation in reconciliation in the modern political climate.

The preservation of victim consciousness in Japan's social, racial, and psychological narratives continues. As the only country to have ever experienced atomic bombings, Japan has made clear its stance towards denuclearization in the Asia-Pacific region. The country's selective reconstruction of war memory has in turn influenced its diplomatic stance regarding nuclear issues.

Contemporary Legacies

Memorials such as the Hiroshima Peace Museum and the Nagasaki Atomic Bomb Museum are can provide insight into how Japan culturally perceives its role in nuclear warfare. The increasing generational gap between hibakusha and their descendants isolates the meaning of commemoration from the politics of memory. Historical distortion of atomic bomb narratives resonates in the approximation of events within these spaces. Focus on the hibakusha and a lack of context for their stories paints the United States as the chief aggressor and fails to recognize the events that preceded the atomic bombings, particularly Pearl Harbor (Schafer 155).

Thus, characterizing the bombs as an example of American dehumanization and placing them at the centerpiece of each memorial in the denial of Japanese militarism has become a way for Japan to claim a pacifist identity in matters such as nuclear disarmament in North Korea and less liability for their previous actions in the Pacific War. As a center for collective memory, commemorations of what happened in Hiroshima and Nagasaki have prioritized narratives that are true, but do not consider Japan's own role in the Pacific War.

Victim consciousness in the literary coverage of the atomic bombings endures in contemporary U.S.-Japan relations. Yet it is imperative to understand the future of denuclearization not through a lens of victimization, but accountability. Instead of portraying itself as the victim, Japan must take into account its acts of aggression in the pre-war period and accept its role in wartime to support its current stance against it. Only when this willingness to acknowledge the place of historical responsibility in the present is realized can the United States and Japan effectively pursue peace and conflict resolution in the Asia-Pacific region today.

Braun, Steven. "Atomic Narratives: U.S. and Japanese Textbook Accounts of Hiroshima and Nagasaki." http://www.stevengbraun.com/atomic-narratives.

Dower, John W. Ways of Forgetting, Ways of Remembering: Japan in the Modern World. New Press, 2014, p. 144.

Glosserman, Brad. "Victimhood in the National Psyche." The Japan Times. 12 Aug. 2001, https://www.japantimes.co.jp/culture/2001/08/12/books/book-reviews/victimhood-in-the-national-psyche/#.WyGiYDOZMU0.

Ham, Paul. "The Bureaucrats Who Singled Out Hiroshima for Destruction." The Atlantic, Atlantic Media Company, 6 Aug. 2015,

https://www.theatlantic.com/international/archive/2015/08/hiroshima-nagasaki-atomic-bomb-anniversary/400448.

Halstead, Fred. "Hiroshima 1945: Behind The U.S. Atom Bomb Atrocity." Emmanuel W. Vedrine, Haiti and the Destruction of Nature, The Militant, 14 Aug. 1995,

www.hartford-hwp.com/archives/20/043.html.

Hara, Tamiki. "Tamiki Hara: Poetry." Voices Education Project.

http://voiceseducation.org/content/tamiki-hara-japanese.

"Hiroshima Archives." Hiroshima Archive. http://hiroshima.mapping.jp/index_en.html.

Naito, Edo. "Patriotism and Nationalism in Postwar Japan." The Japan Times, Yukiko Ogasawara, 3 Sept. 2016,

https://www.japantimes.co.jp/opinion/2016/09/03/reader-mail/patriotism-nationalism-postwar-japan/#.WyGkDzOZMU0.

Orr, James J. The Victim as Hero: Ideologies of Peace and National Identity in Postwar Japan. University of Hawai'i Press, 2001, p. 17.

Seaton, Philip A. Japan's Contested War Memories: The "Memory Rifts" in Historical Consciousness of World War II. Routledge, 2010, p. 41.

Schafer, Stefanie. The Hiroshima Peace Memorial Museum and its Exhibition, Sven and Schwentker, Wolfgang ed. 157-158, p. 155.

Tachibana, Reiko. Narrative as Counter-Memory: A Half-Century of Postwar Writing in Germany and Japan. State University of New York Press, 1998, p. 197.

Tan, Daniela. "Literature and the Trauma of Hiroshima and Nagasaki." Asia Pacific Journal: Japan Focus, vol. 12, no. 40, ser. 3, 2 Oct. 2014.

Treat, John Whittier. Writing Ground Zero: Japanese Literature and the Atomic Bomb. Univ. of Chicago Press, 1995, p. 46.

Yang, Tim. "The Malleable Yet Undying Nature of the Yellow Peril." Dartmouth College.

http://www.dartmouth.edu/~hist32/History/S22%20-The%20Malleable%20Yet%20Undying%20Nature%20of%20the%20Yellow%20Peril.htm.

JOURNALISM

K-Pop stars are redefining mainstream for Asian American youth

Published in *Mercury News*.

For Asian American youth, K-Pop's global popularity is something we've been waiting for.

In the predominantly Asian community of Cupertino where I grew up, second-generation immigrants felt disconnected from our cultures. Asian parents insisted that we should achieve academic excellence before we could examine our heritages. With no representation in American media, we turned to K-Pop — a genre of South Korean music characterized by its use of audiovisual elements — to find people who looked like us: our idols represented us in ways that mainstream American music did not.

BTS — a seven-member boy band — is a K-Pop group that has become a symbol of diversity in the music industry. Much of their music is influenced by a variety of genres, including hip hop, rock and R&B. They've become widely known in the industry for their lyrics about social issues, including mental health, female empowerment and income inequality.

The group's numbers are unprecedented: their album "Love Yourself: Tear" peaked at No. 1 on the U.S. Billboard 200 chart, a first for a Korean-language album; their songs have been downloaded more than

1.6 million times in the United States alone; and they were the first Korean group to perform at the Billboard Music Awards as well as win "Top Social Artist" two years in a row.

Critics of BTS are quick to dismiss their success as a strange phenomenon. What many don't realize is that since the group's debut in 2013, its global fan base has played a key role in their rise to the top.

As an Asian American girl living in a society where I often feel my voice is less valuable than others', BTS is much more than just another Korean group. They have taught me that Asians have as much of a chance to be represented, even if we speak a different language or do not embody the dominant "Western" ideals of the music industry.

When an American interviewer takes the time to learn the names of all seven members or when I see a poster of BTS alongside others of Taylor Swift or Kanye West, I am reminded of the fact that BTS has redefined the definition of "mainstream" not only for themselves, but for the entire K-Pop industry and its audience.

To idolize BTS, or K-Pop for that matter, is to acknowledge pop culture outside of America. To understand BTS' success is to appreciate their representation of their Asian audience.

So before immediately dismissing BTS as another K-Pop group attempting to break into the global market, it's worth asking ourselves if we understand the meaning of "going global." The global market is not just the Western market, and groups like BTS are not overly eager to assimilate. Rather, they are bringing their culture into America in spite of racism and xenophobia.

In this sense, the band's rise to the top is more necessary than ever — it teaches the next generation of Asian American youth that we can be visible too. Through a greater appreciation of K-Pop and what it symbolizes, we can enable others to better understand the value of Asian culture, as well as the importance of keeping it alive.

In Silicon Valley, a Formation of Japanese Identity: Art, Food, and Resistance

Japanese Identity in Silicon Valley: A Series in Two Parts

Published in *Mercury News* and *Stanford Daily*.

1. ART

Japantown project will provide arts groups with a place of their own

New Creative Center for the Arts 'only contributes to the vibrancy of the area'

For the residents of San Jose's Japantown, a cultural revival is coming.

One of the last three historical Japantowns in the United States, Japantown has faced challenges in sustaining its heritage through cultural activities. Arts organizations struggle with expenses, especially because of the high cost of rent in Silicon Valley.

The Creative Center for the Arts, a key ingredient of the planned Japantown Square Project, aims to address this issue. By providing services for the nonprofit creative sector, the center will serve as an inexpensive space for artists to collaborate and foster ethnic unity. Arts catalyst group Silicon Valley Creates is leading the development of the 52,000 square-foot space, which will be located on North Sixth Street between Jackson and Taylor streets.

The center — which is expected to cost $30 million to build — also will provide affordable space for arts organizations, helping to sustain the identity of the neighborhood for Japantown's diverse residents.

San Jose Taiko — a leading Silicon Valley arts organization dedicated to the Japanese art of taiko drumming — is one of the partners moving into the new space and has played a fundamental role in its development.

San Jose Taiko co-founder Roy Hirabayashi said the goal is to make the center a cultural hub for the neighbors.

"The community at large has been very supportive," he said. "It's a space that benefits them. The center only contributes to the vibrancy of the area."

Leslie Kim, the youth volunteer coordinator at the Japanese American Museum, echoed Hirabayashi's sentiments.

"I think it's really exciting to have a space for having those conversations about culture, especially because having a physical anchor for Japanese-American youth is so important," she said.

San Jose Taiko Executive Director Wisa Uemura said the mission of the 21st century model is to keep the spirit of the community alive. Amidst increasing gentrification in Silicon Valley, projects like Japantown Square maximize creative activity in the area by equipping organizations with the resources they need to effectively engage with residents.

"The idea with this is that we can contribute to the needs of the larger ecosystem," said Uemura, who also serves on the center's planning committee. "When we contribute to the sustainability of Japantown, we're also sustaining a lovely neighborhood and ensuring Japantown's artistic vitality. We want to be a part of the fabric, not tear it apart."

The center serves as a symbol of Japantown's history, as well. After the incarceration of Japanese-Americans during World War II, the neighborhood's residents have honored the collective spirit represented in the center's creation.

"From internment, we learned how to make the most of what we have together," Uemura said. "It's something that still lasts today."

Although much of the preliminary development is finished, fundraising and actual construction of the complex remains to be done. The center is expected to be completed in 2020.

"I think what I want people to know about this project is that this new center will really generate interest in not just Japantown, but the larger community," Hirabayashi said. "It's been a long time coming."

2. FOOD

Japanese hit restaurant Ramen Nagi arrives in Palo Alto

Japan's acclaimed ramen chain opens its first U.S. location on Bryant Street

Japanese restaurant Ramen Nagi has opened in Palo Alto, the first U.S. location of the acclaimed ramen chain.

Located at 541 Bryant Street, which formerly housed the Zucca European Restaurant, the new Palo Alto branch is the latest undertaking of the Ko Hospitality Group — Ramen Nagi's US business partner — and the brand itself, which currently has over 35 locations across Asia.

Founded by Chef Satoshi Ikuta in 2004, Ramen Nagi started in bar space that Ikuta borrowed to run a guerrilla ramen restaurant. It became more popular after Ikuta won a contest for a spot in Tokyo's famous Tachikawa Square Park. Since then, the brand has become established for its varied flavor profiles and customizable menu.

According to statements from the Ko Hospitality Group, the decision to expand to the Bay Area comes from a preference for its unique culinary landscape and a desire to enter the U.S. market. A San Jose location is set to open later this summer.

As the president of Ko Hospitality Group, Stanley Ko has played a key role in bringing Ramen Nagi to the United States.

When asked what distinguishes the brand from others, Ko said, "Ramen Nagi doesn't cut corners." The restaurant is well-known for stewing its pork broth for over 20 hours, as well as creating special bowls to retain heat and produce "quality ramen."

"The ramen-making process really takes a lot of time and effort. Bay Area residents are very cosmopolitan and multicultural, and I think that when they're exposed to authentic ramen, then they'll acknowledge that and be appreciative of it," said Ko.

Many of the restaurant's customers have echoed these positive sentiments. First-timer Annie Shiau described her overall experience at Ramen Nagi to be "great" and expects it to become a regular with locals.

"The concept's both unique and interesting, and I think [Ramen Nagi] will definitely connect [Stanford] students one bowl at a time," said Shiau. "It's a great addition to the neighborhood."

Adrienne Hamrah, who dined at Ramen Nagi during its soft opening, said, "Ramen Nagi strikes a balance between original ramen and creative fusion flavors. The core techniques are very authentic in the way they make the soup base and the consistency of the noodles ... to me it's one of the best ramen spots in the Bay Area right now."

But according to Hamrah, one challenge that the restaurant could address is the service, as she felt "rushed" during her dining experience and that bowls were cleared "aggressively" at times to make room for incoming customers.

Hamrah said that while it wasn't uncommon for this to occur with most ramen restaurants, it left her with an impression that it was difficult for the restaurant to manage its long line of patrons.

Whitney Francis (Stanford University '19) also stated that she was less likely to visit a restaurant with a long wait time, no matter how "authentic."

"Thirty minutes is fine with me," she said, before adding, "any more than that and I don't think I could take it."

Yet Francis believes that the mission of Ramen Nagi — which in the words of Ikuta, is to "connect the world through ramen culture" — can help educate others about Japanese culture.

"I want people to know that Japan isn't just sushi and anime, and authentic ramen's a part of that," said Francis, who is half-Japanese and a member of Stanford's Japanese Student Union. "Food is always a good way to connect people, and Japanese culture is really about good food. It's in the taste and flavor. That's how we bring real Japanese values to Palo Alto."

For Ko, the hope is not only to bring existing traditions, but also to create connections between them and the neighborhood at large.

"The reception so far has been great. Everyone's been very warm and welcoming," Ko said. "It's an honor to meet and serve the community. What we really want to do is fulfill everyone's expectations and make Palo Alto residents proud."

Come fall, Boba Guys to open in Town and Country

Milk tea chain emphasizes organic ingredients

Published in *Stanford Daily*.

Boba Guys, a popular milk tea chain known for its unique flavors, will open in Palo Alto's Town & Country Village shopping center this fall.

According to co-founder Andrew Chau, motivation for opening the new Palo Alto location came from widespread customer interest and a desire to continue the growth of the brand.

"I think [people in] Palo Alto and Stanford are really into social justice, about what to do beyond yourself and what to do for the community," said Chau. "And that's really what Boba Guys is all about too ... what we care about is changing cultures and bridging cultures."

As reported by the brand's website, Boba Guys caters not only to the Asian community, but to all communities. So far, it claims to have "introduced boba milk tea to more people than most shops in the entire world."

Expanding Boba Guys to Palo Alto embodies the city's entrepreneurial spirit, according to Chau, as new drinks will be customized specifically for the location.

Yet despite moving into a crowded market — Palo Alto is already home to five other boba shops — Boba Guys claims that its experience is unique from others.

Boba Guys advertises its exclusive use of organic ingredients. According to Chau, the brand's key marketing ingredient is the use of real tea leaves, organic milk and house-made syrups.

Vivian Xiao '19, co-chair of Stanford's Taiwanese Cultural Society, believes that Boba Guys offers a non-traditional approach to boba that will prove popular with Stanford audiences.

"I think that a lot of Stanford students would be willing to switch to Boba Guys," said Xiao, whose favorite boba shops are currently Sharetea on Bryant Street and Teaspoon on Middlefield Road. "It's pretty convenient in terms of location and it's really good quality ... I'm excited for its opening."

Vivian Young, who graduated from Palo Alto High this spring and is a frequent T4 customer, echoed Xiao's sentiments.

"I would definitely pay a little more for Boba Guys' ingredients, so it's really great that they're expanding," Young said. "There's a lot of hype about it on Instagram, so I have a feeling it's going to be super popular."

However, others believe that Boba Guys will be only a novelty, and that the hype will be short-lived.

"I know that Boba Guys is actively trying to produce more unique flavors rather than classic boba milk tea," Rosalie Chang '19 said. "It'll appeal to millennial audiences at Stanford who like using social media, which is good for publicity, but my opinion is that it won't be a staple. To me sugar is just sugar, no matter which form it's in."

Chang expressed a preference for more "authentic" Taiwanese milk drinks, such as plum boba tea and date milk tea.

Xiao and Young said that Boba Guys could offer more special incentives to Stanford and Palo Alto High students for increased attention. For example, Sharetea, located in downtown Palo Alto, offers a 10 percent student discount. For a more competitive edge, Boba Guys' Palo Alto location could also localize their brand by providing benefits for students, the students said.

And according to Chau, these deals are especially relevant to the brand's mission — establishing community.

"People really engage with us more because of the dedication we have to storytelling," Chau said. "Unlike other boba shops, we make an effort to get involved in the community. Boba Guys is our way of having people understand each other a little more."

Each store provides brief narratives on the origins of drink ingredients and sourcing. The two founders also run the Loose Leaf Podcast about their own experiments with tea-making.

According to their website, Boba Guys wants to "change the way people see boba and tea" through healthy endeavors. For Palo Alto residents, the opening of Boba Guys means greater accessibility to nutrition in the brand's exclusive use of organic ingredients. Chau hopes that Boba Guys will play a key role in the appreciation of artisanal boba.

"Boba Guys is the future," Chau said. "What we're trying to uphold is really our interpretation of the modern world."

SHORT STORY

Phonetics

I.

Phonics is good, great. Pronounce the word "cat" like "cat," say the word "dog" like "dog." You can practice phonics by reading Peter Rabbit out loud, but phonics is different from grammar, so don't get the two confused. If you learn phonics, you'll have to start with the Hooked on Phonics books, which is a series. You pronounce "series" like "see-rees." Sometimes, the way you spell out how a word sounds is different from the word itself. Sometimes, the letters that make up a word have different sounds individually, but combined they're all the same. If they're combined, there's only one way to pronounce them.

Mimi's book on phonics has seven different words: cat, hat, rat, mat, sat, fat, shat. (Teacher said that the last one is a mistake, you pronounce mistake like mis-take, which is the same as how the word is spelled.) Her class is called ESL, which stands for "English as a Second Language." Mimi doesn't really know what it means, but her mother says it doesn't matter. It's education, and education is good, and they came here all the way from China for education, so be grateful and appreciate what we sacrificed for you, okay? in Chinese, of course. Mimi's last name is Zhang, but no one can pronounce it correctly. When it's time for roll call, the others pull up their eyes when it's Mimi's turn to say "here." ("Here" is so hard to pronounce, though, that Mimi says "present" instead, and the kids laugh. It's not that funny.)

It's okay, though, because phonics is difficult. All the other kids in the third grade speak English at home, but she does not. Whenever she speaks, her tongue feels hot and heavy. Her throat burns.

Mimi likes math, which is easy to pronounce, except the "th." It's like the rocks she stumbles upon when she's running through the sand pit on the playground, the final hurdle that she just can't cross. At the other end, all her classmates are jumping and waving, and crawling up the American flag and sliding back down again, and she's back at what the other kids call the "Chopsticks," this hamster wheel that you run on until the ends close in and you have to jump off. Mimi's not so swell at that. She's good at the running part though; she never seems to get tired. But then the sides start getting smaller, and then her foot gets caught. It's just a game, they say, but not really. Mimi's been in America long enough to know that there are two definitions to the word "game": the kind you play, and the kind you hunt.

Sometimes word problems are more difficult, but as long as there's a question at the end, everything can be solved. The way your vowels are formed is different. At night, Mimi practices this with her picture books: "Dog takes one apple. Cat takes two. Don't take three, take four." It's almost like the way you curve your fingers over the piano; you cup your hand around a tennis ball and play. Mimi imagines words as apples, as tangible objects that her mouth can form around. Consonants are easy, but vowels are harder.

Mimi lives in Chinatown in San Francisco (it's hard to pronounce), and she doesn't really know what everyone's saying all the time (it's Cantonese, her mother chides, as if Mimi would know what that means), but she knows the faces. They're yellow, like her, and they eat rice and talk about being ih-muh-grunts or something like that. They talk about What Happened in Brooklyn, with the Koreans and the grocery store, and say that they don't want anything like that to happen in Chinatown.

Some of them volunteer at Angel Island, just across in Tiburon. When they come back, they don't seem very happy, but Mimi never asks why. They look at her, clutching her Ivy Ling American Girl doll, eying the glossy black hair, the unblinking brown eyes. Then they shake their heads, and pat her on the shoulder without saying anything. After they leave, Mimi just stares as they head to their respective apartments, the neon lights in Chinese flickering up ahead before diminishing completely.

They don't make a sound.

II.

Ivy Ling had first come to the Cheng home in May of twenty-thirteen. It arrived on the front doorstep packaged in a neat cardboard box, arrays of bubble wrap being shoved in the empty parts. Her hair was black, and she was wearing a red qipao. Her eyes were closed.

They'd gotten Ivy for a considerably lesser price than the other American girls had cost: ninety ninety-nine. At first, Mimi had attributed it to the whole "Best Friend" status, but then her mother pointed out that Ruthie Smithens, Kit Kittredge's Best Friend, was still one hundred twenty. So were Emily Bennett, and Elizabeth Cole, and Nellie O'Malley.

"It's because they're all American," her mother had sniffed, "and Ivy Ling isn't."

Mimi had shrugged. It was a doll, and her classmates had dolls. She brought it to school the next day, and her classmates had looked at Ivy, then back at Mimi, as if trying to compare the two. It wasn't until later, that one of the boys in class pointed out that its eyes were slanted and that its skin was yellow that she realized something was wrong. Next to the Tinker Bells, the Barbies, and the Buzz Lightyears, the yellowness stood out.

III.

It is Lunar New Year, but Mimi still has to go to school. She whines, scrunching her nose up the ugly way, and pouts. Her mother scowls. "Ai-ya, how you gonna get husband that way?" She puts Mimi's hair up in buns, the same kind she sees in her United States History textbooks. There are people stabbing at the buns with sticks. Hopefully, though, that doesn't happen to her. Americans must be kinder than that.

Word problems start being introduced in class that day, and they're by far the hardest part of math, because the thing is that Mimi doesn't know why Julia has seven apples, or how Ben is driving sixty miles per hour. Who gave her the seven apples? What type of car was it? Other people seem to get it, but she doesn't. She raises her hand, and the teacher comes over to help her, but not before saying, "I thought people like you were supposed to be good at math." Ms. Miller gives Mimi a conspiratorial wink, as if they're both in on a secret. Mimi doesn't know what that secret is. It's so hard to understand sometimes.

How do you say Asian? A-sian. So that means As, but there are more letters to the alphabet than that. It's a problem she can't solve.

Mimi thinks, makes up her own word problem: there are seventeen students in math class. Sixteen of them have blue eyes. One has brown eyes. If you subtract the one with brown eyes from the seventeen, how many are left? It should be an easy problem, but it's not. You also have to count the eyes.

III.

When Mimi went back to Beijing last summer, the language felt fuzzy to her, was heavy on her tongue. When her grandparents asked her how the food was, she tried to say that it was terrible, there was barely any rice. The words, when they came out, sounded muffled to her ears. The phonetics were all wrong. Her grandparents smiled and nodded and pretended to understand because back when Mimi lived in Beijing, she'd been the smartest girl around. Her grandparents called her the pride of their generation--a name significant because her grandparents had survived the Cultural Revolution and knew what pride was, knew what bravery was and said being an immigrant was part of it. All the boys were jealous because her name was always there, ranked first. She was a star, golden--the same kind that students in America received on their English papers and she didn't.

Back then, she hadn't been just Mimi Ching Chong Ching Chong. She was Zhang Mei-ying, with beautiful in the middle and silver in the last syllable. Whenever she pronounced her name, she made sure that her tongue was suck to the back of her front teeth. It sounded more intelligent that way.

But when she came back after living in America for so long, there was a language barrier —thin, but still there. Her grandparents chattered and laughed and ate their noodles, reached over for the fish. Whenever Mimi listened to them, she could practically taste her native language, but it only lingered before it was gone completely. When her grandmother spoke about the time at the market when Mrs. Pao had bumped into her, knocking her pork sauce and bok choy right out of her hands, Mimi wanted to say that Mrs. Pao had always been that way. The pinyin — English spelling — was there, but not the tones. It sounded like gibberish. Her grandparents smiled and nodded, but behind their eyes she could just see the shadow of disappointment.

When Mimi arrived back to the flat in Chinatown, there was this sense that she wasn't really Chinese. There were so many stories to tell, and she didn't even know how to say them. She tried, she really did. She just couldn't get the sounds right.

IV.

She'd liked the sound of America before she'd come. When she read about the United States in her World History textbook, it'd seemed like such a great place. All those smiling white people, a good education.

It wasn't until later that she realized: sometimes, the colors and letters that make up a word have different sounds individually, but combined they're all the same. If they're combined, there's only one way to pronounce them. That way wasn't the way she thought it was.

V.

Home is a funny concept. In Chinese, home is jia. Open mouth, freedom. When you say home in English, your mouth forms a smaller "o" shape. It's easy getting mixed up in all the phonics of it. It's just like running the hamster wheel, when the ends close in and you have to jump off. The sides are too small. Freedom gets caught.

Sometimes she can't even think back to why she came to this country at all. Other times, she does. Mimi came for the sounds: liberty, equality, democracy. She came for the sound: America, home of the free and land of the brave. America. America.

When she says the word, it feels bitter around the edges.

www.ingramcontent.com/pod-product-compliance
Lightning Source LLC
Chambersburg PA
CBHW021217020426
42331CB00003B/354